I Am A Miracle

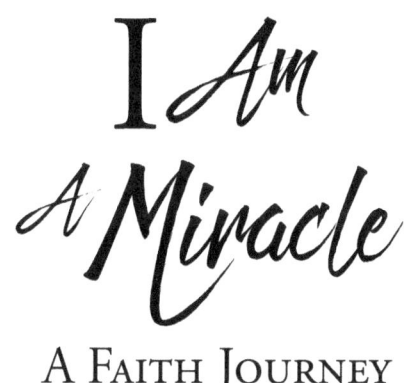

A Faith Journey

Christine Morris

XULON PRESS

Xulon Press
2301 Lucien Way #415
Maitland, FL 32751
407.339.4217
www.xulonpress.com

© 2019 by Christine Morris

All rights reserved solely by the author. The author guarantees all contents are original and do not infringe upon the legal rights of any other person or work. No part of this book may be reproduced in any form without the permission of the author. The views expressed in this book are not necessarily those of the publisher.

Scripture quotations taken from the King James Version (KJV) – *public domain.*

Printed in the United States of America.

ISBN-13: 9781545679098

Table of Contents

Introduction ix
Chapter 1: Starch Baby 1
Chapter 2: Heart Attack. 5
Chapter 3: Set Back 9
Chapter 4: Surgery. 13
Chapter 5: Stroke. 19
Chapter 6: Rehabilitation 25
Chapter 7: His Life Today. 29
Chapter 8: My Experience as a Wife 31

Introduction

Dr. Felton L. Morris, Jr. praises the Lord for the opportunity to bless others with the telling of his miraculous story. He is blessed to boast about the goodness of the Almighty, knowing that without God, he can do nothing; the Lord is always with him. He has read about different men, women, and children who were healed miraculously in the Bible. Now, allowed the telling of his story, he shares how Jesus became his Great Physician and why all of the glory belongs to God.

While going through his trials and tribulations, Felton learned more about his purpose by surrendering to the Lord and showing and expressing His love more than ever. His compassion is significant towards everyone, and he is reaching out to all he can.

Dr. Felton L. Morris, Jr. is a man of purpose, knowledge, acknowledgment, and is learning to not lean on his understanding; he trusts in the Lord (Prov. 3:5-6). He wants everyone to know that it's not about him; it's about the Lord. Felton gives the Lord all the glory for bringing him through a scary ordeal. He very distinctly informs us that God is real, and continually thanks and praises God for the prayers He answered on his behalf.

> "I will bless the Lord at all times:
> his praise shall continually be in my mouth."
> (Psalm 34:1)

Felton has had a miraculous healing. Although he has been through several experiences relating to his health, he always managed to stay positive while encouraging others. At first, he did not wanting to believe and accept his initial medical report, and it is from this experience that he has learned to check and examine both his spiritual and physical lives, since both convey messages. "It's important to pay attention to your spirit and your body!" Felton says. He likes to express how significant it is to "come to meet a man" (John 4:29). That man is Jesus!

> "O, taste and see that the Lord is good;
> Blessed is the one who takes refuge in Him!"
> (Psalms 34:8)

Chapter 1

Starch Baby

While growing up, no one knows God's plan for himself, but we all have a purpose. From the day of his birth, he was favored by God.

Felton came into this world on the sixteenth day of October in 1945, born to Annie L. Hamilton, in Trenton, New Jersey. As he grew, his mother told him that he was a blessed baby. During those days, African American women liked to eat boxes of starch – Argo Starch. His mother craved it all day long and had eaten so much of it, that when he was born, the doctor had to scrape the starch off of his skin and immediately applied Vaseline because of its dryness. It was through his mother's prayers and the daily medical regimen of using Vaseline that he received healing and was able to leave the hospital to go home after two weeks. He was a tiny baby, too, so they carried him around on a pillow.

As a little boy, he attended church every Sunday with his mother and grandmother and took part in the Sunday school. It was there he learned about the Lord. When Felton grew and got older, he was able to play with the children in the neighborhood of Friendly Park. Eventually, he grew to become a young man at the height of 5'11".

When Felton attended Blanche Ely High School, located in Pompano Beach, Florida, he was chosen to play basketball. His role as a forward on the team allowed him to contribute in any way possible. He enjoyed playing basketball, but unfortunately, one night had a nasty fall. As a consequence, he hit his head and suffered a concussion. Later that evening, he went to the hospital to be examined and was admitted overnight. Through prayer and trusting in the Lord, God brought him through it again. Because of his swift recovery, Felton was able to continue playing at Blanche Ely and got better at the game. Fortunately for him, he received a scholarship to play at Morgan State College in Baltimore, Maryland.

After a year in college, Felton decided to go to New Jersey to see his Uncle Dut and extended family. He stayed longer than expected, enjoying the time he spent with relatives, eventually returning home to Florida. But, a few weeks after this move, Uncle Sam found out Felton was no longer in school and drafted him into the Army on July 11, 1967. He went to Columbus, Georgia and completed basic training in six weeks; and he returned home for a month on leave. When he returned to duty, Felton went to Lake Charles, Louisiana for combat training, and his work assignment was as a supply clerk. After completing combat training, he was moved to Oakland, California to receive his immunizations before heading to Long Binh, Vietnam.

When Felton arrived in Long Binh, he pulled guard duty for six weeks, before receiving a job at the PX (commissary). He would pick up the mail from the airport and do mail call every day. At the time, he was unaware that he was receiving experience for his future career as a mail carrier.

When first drafted into the army, Felton was terrified. He prayed and asked the Lord to help him to serve his country and make it back home safely. His prayer was, "Lord, I'll do anything you want me to do." In the combat zone, it was normal for shootings to happen that resulted in many of his army buddies being killed. But the Lord protected him, and he was able to come home alive in February of 1969. Thank you, Jesus!

On September sixth of 1973, Felton and I wed. We are blessed to have four children; three girls – Sonya, Sherry, and LaToya – and one boy, Felton, III. At this writing, we have fifteen grandchildren; two of our grandsons have passed on. We are a loving and devoted family, and Felton is highly respected by all of his children and extended family members.

CHAPTER 2

Heart Attack

One night, Felton and I were attending a revival meeting at Word of Living God in Pompano Beach led by Pastor John Mohorn. During the time of prayer, he was called up by Elder R. Gilliard, who was the revivalist. Elder R. Gilliard asked him if he had any pains, and he answered, "No." The elder put his hands on Felton and told him that he was going to have a heart attack, but God was going to bring him through it. The more Elder R. Gilliard talked about the pain in his heart, the more it affected me. Felton didn't know that I had been feeling his pains in my own body, but I told him about it later.

After this meeting, Felton continued with his usual routine and gave no more thought to what Elder R. Gilliard had spoken to him. His daily routine was getting up every morning and praying, reading from his prayer book, and watering the grass before going to work. While working his mail route, he would often sit in the air-conditioned van. One day, however, while delivering mail, he began to get extremely hot and experienced shortness of breath. He wondered why he was sweating so profusely and called to tell me what he was experiencing. I said, "It sounds like you're having a slight heart attack." He ignored my response. He thought he was just too hot from working.

On another day, he was tending the yard, using the weed cutter at the time, when he started to hurt badly. The pain hit him harder than what he experienced while delivering mail. He laid the weed cutter down and went inside the house to rest. When I came in and saw him, I asked what was wrong. He told me that he was hurting on his left side; that it was hurting badly, but eventually, the pain eased up. I began to observe him more closely.

We went to church the Sunday following the second event of his chest pain. While there, Felton was singing very happily with our granddaughter, Tabria, and our son, Felton, III, who was playing the music to "He's Been Good to Me" by Lee Williams. He preached that Sunday, but when he came home, he was feeling so bad that he climbed into bed, laid down, and stayed there until the next morning. That morning, I went to take the grand kids to school. While gone, he got up, prayed for himself, and put oil everywhere, but he was still hurting. When I returned home, I asked, "What's wrong? Do you want me to take you to the doctor?" He told me, "No, I'll take myself."

Felton drove three miles to Northwest Medical Center in Margate. When he parked the car, he got out and was walking from the front to the back, not knowing exactly how to get into the emergency room. Finally, he made it into the emergency room and, for about ten minutes, waited before he saw the doctor. When the nurse attendant asked him to describe his symptoms, he told the nurse that he was having sharp pains. When asked what his pain level was on a scale of one to ten, he said it was a one, but the attendant stated it was a ten. Immediately, the staff took him to the back area while telling him that he had a heart attack.

Continuing with their examination, they asked him what medications he was taking. He said to them that he only drank Tahitian Noni® juice. Our family has taken Tahitian Noni® juice for about nine years. The nurses double-checked that he was taking no other medications, and he responded, "That's it." We were thankful to the Lord, and for Noni, because that's what held Felton - God's power and Tahitian Noni®.

While he was being admitted, I called him. When he answered the phone, I stated, "You haven't called me." He responded, "I've had a heart attack." His cousin, Carolyn, who worked at the hospital emergency room, took his phone and told me what was going on. They prepared him for emergency surgery to place stents in his groin. I went immediately to the hospital, and other family members joined me there. While the procedure was going on, we all gathered in the waiting room, praying while waiting, and the procedure was a success.

Chapter 3

Set Back

Every evening, my cousin Carolyn, Felton, and I would go for a walk at the park. Usually, we would all start out together, but this time he was a little slow. Carolyn and I walked ahead of him for a distance, while talking and laughing. I looked back and asked him, "Are you coming?" He answered, "I'll be on." But he never caught up and eventually gave up because of the pain he was experiencing. He was sweating and started to have mild pains to come and go, similar to when he initially had the heart attack. So, he sat down while Carolyn and I finished our walk. He told us that he was hurting and would just sit and wait for us to finish. When we did, we all went home. Felton discussed with me what was happening to him, and decided to make an urgent appointment with his doctor.

The next day, he went to his doctor's office for an examination. The doctor scheduled him to be admitted to the hospital on the following day as an outpatient to run a few tests, but he could go home once the tests were completed. Later, the doctor's office called him to come in and get the results. A few days later, Felton went to his doctor's office, alone, to discuss the findings. When he came home, he reported that the doctor told him that the stents, which were placed in his groin earlier, were no longer supporting his heart, and that was the cause of his recurring pain. Four of his arteries were blocked, and he definitely had heart disease.

The doctor followed with questions: "Did you ever smoke?"

Felton answered, "Yes, for a little."

He asked him, "Have you ever been in the service?"

Again, his answer was, "Yes."

"What branch of the service?"

He informed the doctor that he had been in the army and served in Vietnam. The doctor told Felton that Vietnam was where they sprayed the Agent Orange in the air, and that he was exposed to it, which was now the probable cause for his heart disease. (He received an 18 percent disability rating from the V.A. because of the exposure.) After his discussion with his physician, he was advised to bring me with him for the next visit so that all of us could discuss the procedure.

When we returned to the office a few days later, the doctor told us that Felton did, in fact, have serious heart disease and would have to have a triple bypass. He explained everything about the procedure, and that this was the only measure that could help him at that time. We asked a lot of different questions about the triple bypass surgery, and I turned to Felton and asked, "Is this really what you want?" His answer was, "Yes, because I don't want to continue to hurt, and figured I might as well just get it done." He said he was ready, so we told the doctor - "Let's do this."

The doctor referred us to the heart surgeon, who would actually perform the triple bypass surgery. His receptionist made the appointment for us, and we went to see the surgeon a few days later. He examined Felton to make sure he was a candidate for the surgery. Felton would go back to see him for one appointment before the actual procedure. When we returned for that second visit, the surgeon discussed the details of the triple bypass surgery.

Chapter 4

Surgery

*I*t was the day of surgery. Felton and I left around home around six o'clock in the morning, heading to Florida Medical Center in Lauderdale Lakes, Florida. We had to be there early to pre-op preparations. When the doctors came in the room, they went over everything that would take place during the operation. The surgeon then told our family members what we could expect after the surgery, how to cope, and why we shouldn't be alarmed, because Felton would be okay. The surgical team then came to prepare him for transfer to the surgical suite.

On our way from pre-op to the surgical suite, (our godsister, Linda Walker, walking alongside me), I asked Felton if he was okay. He told me he had to have the surgery and was ready to get it done. So, they took him into surgery, and we went to the surgical waiting room.

When Linda and I went into the waiting room, there we met with my other cousins, Bishop Lonnie and Susie Johnson, and we continued to pray for my husband. While we waited, the surgical staff told me they would keep me updated with how the surgery was proceeding, and how my husband was doing. Now, this was where the real trial began: the waiting period.

Waiting perfects patience, because there is nothing you can do about anything but wait. While my husband was in surgery, I was letting the Spirit of the Lord do His work within me. I was in prayer the whole time. There were a lot of people around who were smiling and talking, but I wasn't engaged in a lot of talking. I was just sitting and staying in tune with the Lord while the surgery continued. The hospital staff was very nice to me through the waiting; they came to me after about an hour to let me know that the surgery had begun and how things were going so far.

All of my children called and checked-in on me and let me know they would be there when they got off work. The staff reported to me a second time, letting me know the surgery was finished, everything was going well, and someone would be in soon to speak with me. Shortly thereafter, a nurse came in and asked, "Who is Mrs. Morris?"

I answered, "I am."

She said, "Everything went fine; the surgery is finished. They're putting his heart back in right now as we speak." I was thankful and, at the same time, taken aback by what she said to me. She probably saw my expression and went on to say, "They took the heart out, sat it on the table, and put it on potassium to keep it."

I told her, "Thank you."

She then told me they would call me when they brought him to the ICU. When they completed the process, he was taken to the ICU unit, and they called for me to come see him.

When I looked upon Felton, he was as they described, but his eyes were also a little puffy. The medical attendants kept saying how well he came through. When the children arrived and saw him, they started crying because of how he looked. I was aware of what to expect because the staff had already explained to me what his appearance would be. I was surprised by their crying out, "Look at my daddy!" Look at my daddy!" They were acting like he was dying and telling me, "You are just strong, Mama." I spoke to LaToya, and Sally spoke to Sherry, and they calmed down. I was more interested in Felton, so I asked him how he was doing. He responded by shaking or nodding his head, showing me he understood what I was asking, and I was reassured that he was okay.

They allowed me sit awhile with him but told me that I could not spend the night and would have to come back in the morning. I told Felton I would be back then, and I left. On my way home, I was praying and listening to my favorite Clarke Sisters album.

On my first night at home without Felton, my niece, Lois, stayed with me. I was still processing all that had happened: the heart attacks and the two surgeries, but I refused to worry too much. I went to my source, the Lord, and talked to Him. I first thanked Him and let Him know that my husband, my family, and I appreciated Him for His goodness toward us. Yes, my husband could have died from the heart attacks, but he walked around and carried on, tolerating the pain. I then petitioned to know of the Lord if my husband would make it all the way through, because I missed him already.

As I was sitting there in my living room, I received a visitation from an angel. It was so shiny, pretty and white (beyond a silky white), standing at my front door. The angel let me know that everything was well, and then it vanished. When the angel disappeared, I didn't say a word, and in my spirit, I had received the answer. I just praised and thanked the Lord some more. All the glory goes to God! He is worthy, and He's the one who watched over my husband while he was in the hospital.

The day was coming to a close while I sat on the couch, contemplating, and eventually, I fell asleep. A few hours later, I got up and started preparing for my visit, anxiously looking forward to seeing my husband. When I arrived at the hospital, I went in to see him, and he was already looking better and doing better, according to the nurses. They were saying how he was recovering so fast and how unusual it was. My husband told them how the Noni® Juice helps with his system.

On a side note, let me tell you a little about Tahitian Noni® Juice. Our family has been drinking the dietary supplement for more than a decade. It's packed with vitamins, minerals, antioxidants, and anti-inflammatory properties. It's often referred to as a "superfruit" and a "wonder food" because it is packed with nutritional benefits for the body. It comes from the noni plant, which is in the coffee family, and is often mixed with grape juice to tolerate the bitter taste of it. The Tahitian Noni® Juice is a family staple in the Morris home.

Chapter 5

Stroke

Several months after the surgery, we were traveling to visit our grandson, who was in college near Orlando, Florida. My husband got very confused trying to use the GPS to get us back on track. Courtney, our grandson, had already given us the directions, but he spoke to me; when I tried to give directions, Felton answered by yelling at me, "I'm driving this car!" I looked at him, because he sounded so angry and the tone in which he spoke to me. I said, "Felt, you didn't have to yell at me so loud. I was only trying to help you." That was unusual for him. Afterward, it became very quiet as we traveled along. He finally calmed himself down and got into the right lane. Felton would always say that I have the wisdom to get us back on track. So, we continued to follow the directions that Courtney had given us, which led us directly to his home.

During the night, I kept watching him and praying. There was something going on with him that wasn't right. The way he was moving in his sleep wasn't normal, and the sounds he was making were unusual. I had never heard sounds like what I was now hearing while he slept. He got up one time and went to the bathroom; then he came back to bed and went to sleep again.

He got up the next morning, asking, "Where is the bag with my toothbrush and all of my belongings?" I answered him, "I don't know. That's unusual. You always bring the bags out of the car. Let's check the car to see if it's there." We went back to the car and saw that the bags were there. Now that we had found his toiletry bag, we began getting ready to leave Courtney to go back home.

Once we got back on the road and were headed toward the turnpike, my husband was speeding. He didn't say anything at first, but I later asked, "Why are you driving so fast? I guess you really got to get home, huh?" I asked, "Are you alright?" and he said, "Yes." Riding along the highway, I was praying for him. A person acting like he was is either dying or senses something really bad is going to happen; but, God answered my prayers, and we made it home safe. I thanked the Lord.

When we arrived home, my youngest daughter, LaToya, and her family were at the house getting ready to go to Tabria's birthday party. The girls and I went to the birthday party. My granddaughter, Nene, stayed behind with her mom but would come to the party later. While we were getting ready, Felton left to go to the bank to check our account, like he usually does after a trip. After making sure everything was fine, he headed towards the house.

When Felton reached the house, he turned the car off but couldn't get out of it. He stayed in the driver's seat for two to three minutes and attempted again to get out. This time, he dropped the keys and fell to the ground. He doesn't remember anything after that. Our next-door neighbor, who observed what happened to him, picked him up off the ground and put him on the chair, but he was still unconscious. My daughter, LaToya, tried calling me, but she couldn't reach me on the phone. So, she called my daughter-in-law, Tiffany, who said, "Momma, Toya is on the phone, and she is crying and said Daddy fell and he isn't saying anything."

Tiffany handed me the phone, and I asked my daughter, "What's wrong, LaToya?"

She was crying and said, "Mom, Dad fell out! He hasn't come to." I asked her, you know what happened, and if he was hurt? I told her to put her hand on his head and that I was going to pray. I instructed her to put the phone to his ear, while I prayed, and I began to pray for him.

While praying, Toya brought the phone back to her ear and said, "Mom, he is coming back to now.

I said, "Thank you, Jesus," and, "I'm on my way." My son and I left the party and went home, while my son-in-law followed us.

When we got there, the neighbor said, "Y'all beat the rescue wagon," and then we all began to laugh. Before too long, there was my husband sitting in the back of the rescue wagon, looking. The paramedics asked him if he knew me, and he answered, yes and that I was his wife. They took him to the hospital, and we all followed. He was sitting on the bed, and his right side was not functioning. They examined him and said everything was fine, and it a blessing that he got there in time, because if he hadn't within that hour, he would have died. The doctor was also a Christian, and he really believed in the Lord. He told me and my children, "You don't want him to be a vegetable or where he can't walk on that side."

After a thorough examination of Felton, the doctor said he was a candidate for a medicine they wanted to use. Only one person had used this medicine previously, and it was a young girl. The doctor also suggested that my husband get the medicine within that hour and assured us his vital signs were all good. My children and I decided we would go with the medicine they had. The next doctor was a young lady. She came in for me to sign the papers. By the time I did, I saw the doctor going into the room with Felton.

Following the emergency treatment, Felton was able to move his arms, legs, and everything. We were excited and blessed the Lord. This medication, they explained to us, was just like using Drano® for a clogged drain; it cleared the brain blockage. Once the blockage was released, Felton felt much better. He was then transferred to an inpatient room, and when we got there, he was sitting up in the bed with the remote in his hands, changing the TV channels and looking like himself.

Chapter 6

Rehabilitation

Rehabilitation is a process, as we know, to restore our health. My husband and I experienced his rehabilitation training together. Therapy helped with the different exercises he would do on a daily basis. Along with the exercises, the rehabilitation regimen also included taking medicine and eating right; he was placed on a special diet. As his strength returned, and he got better, he was able to go back to work, as long as he followed the orders from the doctor. But when he started working again, the pain returned, this time more severely than the first. Since the pain was worse, he went back to the doctor for another examination to diagnose the problem.

Since he had the groin surgery, and later the triple bypass surgery, Felton had to begin a more intense phase of therapy. He would have to sit for hours on a couch to start his healing process. It was not easy; he said the pains were sharp and felt like gas. Other times, he described the pain as a "balled-up fist in his chest," because it had tightened up so bad on him. However, the daily therapy regimen with the therapists and nurses aided him in recovery, and he began to improve rather quickly. He would not be able to return to work.

Because the doctors stated that Felton could not return to work, shortly after that, he retired. His retirement meant that he would no longer have medical coverage to cover his therapeutic home visits; therefore, he would have to attend his weekly therapy at the V.A. clinic.

His health continued to improve tremendously, and now he is doing much better. He also continued with the speech therapy at the V.A. clinic for his speech to return. He always took his prayer book with him because he believed that he could overcome anything with the help of God. With the help of the prayer book, his speech started to come back little by little. He got so much better with speaking; he talked too fast. I had to tell him to slow down, so I could understand what he was saying. He was so excited!

Felton used the prayers for deliverance and healing. He always looked forward to his speech and physical therapy sessions because he was able to tell others about his battles and how the Lord had brought him through everything. Some of the other individuals at the V.A. could not walk or talk like him, and some looked to be younger and some older. Seeing his improvement gave the others hope! They looked up to him since he was healing in a fast manner.

After a few weeks at the V.A. clinic, it was time for another checkup, because we were planning to go on a trip. After the examination, he was cleared to travel. My brother, Lenzo, waited with me for the exam to be completed. When Felton came back from the checkup, he told us that he was fine, but we noticed that he looked tired. He stated that he felt good and was happy. After the visit to the doctor, we started planning for our trip.

When we returned from the trip, the symptoms of a stroke began to kick in, and we began to pray. Trusting in the Lord is the best therapy you can have. Always bless Him, and do not forget the source of your benefits. Remember that, "a merry heart doeth good like a medicine" is an excellent therapy (Prov. 17:22). One of my most profound experiences was watching my husband go through having a stroke. I observed him with hawk eyes.

When it first happened, I was sitting in the room. When our daughter's oldest son, David, came in the emergency room, Felton was lying on his back, and he looked up at David with a happy expression, since he hadn't seen him in a long time. My husband was beautiful and shining like he had seen an angel; he was so happy to see David. What I am trying to tell you is that love is the best of therapies. After Felton received his "miracle" shot, he was able to leave the emergency room, since he was doing well.

Our children, grandchildren, and niece were there. Our cousins were in Orlando on a trip, and I had called them. The Watson's prayed with us. Kimmy and Lametra Davis' family came from Orlando to be with us. When he saw his family members, he didn't remember names, but he knew their faces. When Felton saw all of us together, there appeared another glow on his face. Glory to the Lord, he knew who his people were.

During the time that he was in the hospital, his closest friends came and prayed with me. Some of his friends that he referred to as his brothers were: Alonzo, Terry, Carl Lee, and Lonnie; Apostle John Mohorn (a close cousin); Bishop Lonnie Johnson and Pastor O'Neal; and our neighbor, Chris. They all came and prayed with my daughters and me as well. Our church family, supervisor, and his postal coworkers contributed, too.

Thank the Lord always, and continue to stay under the anointing of the Lord. Always remember that there is someone bigger than us!

Chapter 7

His Life Today

My husband is a man of integrity, who respects and honors the Lord. He also appreciates his family and friends. Felton wanted to share his story of how he was a miracle because of all the battles fought and the love of God he experienced. God gave him a second chance because he is a man of purpose. He likes to share his story, to let everyone know that he is blessed: physically and spiritually. And it's not all about him; it is all about our Almighty God.

He was blessed with kind nurses and doctors who cared for him and believed in the Lord. Felton's experiences brought him closer to the Lord. God is real!

"In the beginning, He created the heavens and Earth" (Gen. 1:1).

"God is the Alpha and the Omega and the beginning and end" (Rev. 1:8).

"For God so loved the world he gave his only begotten son, but whosoever believe in him should not perish but have everlasting life" (John 3:16).

Felton is continually giving his Daddy all the glory and praise.

"Bless the Lord, O my soul: and all that is within me, bless His Holy Name" (Ps. 103:1-3).

God brought Felton through for His purpose, and now Felton is using his time wisely. Everywhere he goes, he's telling someone his testimony. He is very blessed because he could not walk or talk, and his eyes were affected after the stroke. But Felton is healed!

It is essential to pay attention to your body because it always sends you messages when something is going wrong. Felton ignored his first experience because he thought he was just hot and could not breathe well. Later, he realized that he just ignored the problem; he was very stubborn. Each day, he kept going about his regular routine until the pain started striking him. Prayer is what kept him going. I want to remind everyone to remember to acknowledge the Lord in everything you do. The Lord is your director and protector, and He will lead you in all the right directions and take you down the right paths.

CHAPTER 8

My Experiences as a Wife

I am Christine Morris, the wife of Felton Morris for forty-five years. I am a woman of purpose, which I have known from my childhood. My dad always told me that I had a calling on my life and, that one day, I would understand what his words meant. In the experience of life, you never know what trials and tribulations you will face. So, it is essential to count your blessings and to be in the Lord. Your flesh cannot handle most experiences alone; knowing this fact is a key to being blessed. You must also have a mindset of kingdom living. I am glad I was able to get exposure to God's graces through the struggles that happened throughout my life.

"Every knee will bow, and every tongue will confess, that Jesus Christ is Lord." (Romans 14:11)

Since the trials of life are hard to bear at most times, you will not be able to carry them alone. My advice is to give God time in prayer and praise and feed your spirit the Word of God, which enables you to be strong while going through the fiery trials that life affords. You are not alone, and He is there when you need Him. One day, every tongue will have to confess that Jesus Christ is Lord, and every knee shall bow to Him, and that should start now.

Battles can hit you really hard, and you must be prepared to fight back. At the time of Felton's trials (heart attack, triple bypass, setbacks, symptoms from the first heart attack that returned, a stroke), if it were not for the grace and mercy of God, I would not have made it. When my husband was going through all those different attacks and procedures, everyone was looking to see how I was reacting and holding up. I was going through with the flow of the spirit; I made it by praying daily. I experienced the Holy Spirit, which is my keeper and my strength, and He is my inner man. I relied wholly on God, and He kept me through it all. It was my consistent faith that kept me going.

"Trust in the Lord with all thine heart, and lean not unto thine own understanding.
In all thy ways acknowledge Him,
and he shall direct thy paths." (Proverbs 3:5-6)

I did not allow negativity to take over, and I realized that I am on God's time. I continue to thank and praise Him every day, and all day, because it is still about Him. He gets all the glory and praise, not us!

Let me add, every woman should seek the Lord for your husband, just like I did. Marriage is serious business. You marry God first then fall in love with Jesus, and it will help you love everyone else. God has to be your priority. He is first in my life; that is why I don't have a problem seeking and talking to Him. When you're done saying your vows, God still has to be first for your marriage to work. Battles will occur, but you will need to rely on God to hold you up.

I was already committed to my husband with the help of God. He allowed me to be happy and to be there for him when needed the most. I just progressed with my spiritual warfare by trusting in the Lord, and we made it through. By the grace of our dear Lord, whom all the glory goes to, we are a man and woman of purpose, and He has kept us for His purpose.

God bless each of you. It is our prayer that our tests and testimonies have inspired you to draw closer to the Lord; to believe that He can do for you more than you can ask or think and that you will place your absolute trust in Him. God still saves; He works miracles of healing, and He delivers from all kinds of situations. Trust Him today!

"No weapon formed against thee shall prosper."
(Isaiah 54:17)

www.ingramcontent.com/pod-product-compliance
Lightning Source LLC
LaVergne TN
LVHW021742060526
838200LV00052B/3422